Holderness
in old picture postcards

by Ben and Mave Chapman

European Library ZALTBOMMEL/THE NETHERLANDS

Acknowledgements
The production of any book is a long and lonely task, though help from other people comes in various forms, be it practical support, snippets of useful information, or simply encouragement. For practical support we would like to thank our niece Jane Conroy for chauffeuring us around to postcard fairs and on research expeditions. Our thanks to our dear friend Muriel Kirk for her loan of photographs and other material, and for sharing her knowledge of the area with us. Most of the illustrations in the book are from the Chapman Social History Archive, though a few important gaps have been filled by the generous loan of photographs from the following people: Catherine Beadle, Jean and Roy Dowling, Mrs. Fussey, Dale Smith, Mrs. Huitt, Bob Parkes and Mr. Lanham.

We would like to acknowledge Wayne Wolton and postcard dealer Barry Rollinson of Rotherham for their support. Our grateful thanks also to the staff of Withernsea Library and the Local History Department of Hull Central Library.

Withernsea 1995, Ben and Mave Chapman

GB ISBN 90 288 6047 9 / CIP
© 1995 European Library – Zaltbommel/The Netherlands

Introduction

The part of the East Riding of Yorkshire designated Holderness is an area of just over 200 square miles. Geographically it is located at the east of the county forming a rough triangle of arable land ranging from the tip of Spurn in the south, along thirty miles of coastline to just above Hornsea in the north. The western boundary touches on the villages of Swine, Bilton and Paull, moving eastwards down the Humber Estuary back to Spurn Point.

The name 'Holderness' taken through its ancient derivations from the eleventh century, is thought to mean 'cape of the High Reeve' a reference to an officer of high rank in the Danelagh. Geologically Holderness is an area of contrasts. It is formed of a variety of glacial and postglacial deposits. It is basically very flat with expanses of boulder clay and features such as winding streams and some marshy hollows. Prone to erosion by the elements and the relentless waves of the North Sea, the low boulder clay cliffs have always suffered the vicissitudes of nature. Since medieval times several villages have been washed away. Coastal erosion is still a contentious issue as some villages and homes are presently endangered, and there is great concern for the future.

Populated by Bronze Age settlers in earlier times, the area is rich in archaeological heritage with many beautiful artifacts on display in local museums. Close to Scandanavia and Northern Europe, Holderness was frequently raided and subsequently settled by these foreign invaders. The Danish influence of the ninth century AD is still apparent with many of the place names. For example, those ending in 'thorpe' indicate a farm or hamlet. Endings of 'ton' and 'by' respectively are taken from the Old Norse of 'tun', a town, and though 'by' has several Old English connotations, it is thought to have derived from the Old Norse, indicating a dwelling place.

The two principle ways of earning a living for Holderness folk were through agriculture and its ancillary trades, or by fishing, both inland and at sea. Being a very fertile region with many villages and only three principal small towns, agriculture and animal husbandry provided a large number of jobs and occupations.

The area being extremely flat and subject to the strong winds blowing in from the North Sea, made it an ideal area for the situation of windmills. Many corn mills were built in Holderness with the trade of milling and its associated services providing not only employment, but also the daily bread for the inhabitants of a very wide area.

The Great Plague or Black Death of 1349 took its toll of the area leaving some places depopulated, thus sounding the death knell of the feudal system. The restriction on the movement of people and the almost catastrophic shortage of workers ensured that a man could sell his labour to the highest bidder.

Fish, an important source of nourishment, was caught off the coast in the North Sea and also in some of the inland meres. These were considered difficult from the point of view of drainage, but did have a commercial value in that they yeilded fish. Burton Pidsea had a fishery, as did Burstwick, and there was an eel pond at Brandesburton. There were meres at Skipsea, Withernsea and Hornsea, the latter at which is the only one now remaining.

The character of the area was enhanced by the gentry who built their big houses in Holderness, a feature being the intensive use of trees in their parklands in a landscape which was otherwise singularly lacking in woodland. The larger of these estates is Burton Constable, the home of the Constable family, which established itself here towards the end of the thirteenth century.

The three principle towns of Holderness are Hedon, Hornsea and Withernsea. Hedon, which is situated near the south-west boundary, is a popular market town, originally a flourishing port visited by ships from many European countries in early medieval times. It lost its prestige as a port when the influential De la Pole family of bankers and traders moved westwards along the River Humber to what is now the port of Kingston upon Hull. The town still maintains much of the medieval plan and is still dominated by the magnificent church dedicated to St. Augustine. The impressive collection of corporation silver includes a beautiful 25 inch long mace thought to be the oldest in England.

Hornsea and Withernsea are popular seaside resorts, Hornsea being the larger. Originally a small village on the banks of the large freshwater lake, the mere, it grew over the years towards the sea and became an attractive town. Hornsea's popularity as a holiday resort was assured when the railway linked Hull with Hornsea in 1864.

Situated on the coast a few miles north of Spurn Point is the seaside town of Withernsea, dominated by its splendid lighthouse which was erected in 1894 and is now the town museum. The modern town of Withernsea also owes its popularity as a seaside resort to the railway which transported many people from nearbye Hull to enjoy the bracing air and wonderful beach with such delightful amenities as donkey rides, children's swings and refreshments. The railway linking Hull and Withernsea was opened in 1854. During the early part of the century and indeed to the present day, both Hornsea and Withernsea have supported small fishing communities, which apart from the traditional fish catches, seasonally lay down crab and lobster pots to augment their earnings.

Even today, in the hustle and bustle of modern living, Holderness has a kind of serenity. Perhaps this is due to large vistas of flat agricultural land under the vast expanse of a sky that reaches into infinity. There is still an air of unhurried life, and friendliness pervading the whole of this unique area.

An added attraction is, of course, the coastline where aspects of the sea can be enjoyed in solitary peace from vantage points such as Spurn and Kilnsea, or at the more robust resorts of Hornsea and Withernsea.

The agricultural aspect which has marked Holderness through the centuries as a special place, is still of great importance, and it is due to this that the people, whilst showing a fierce independence of character along with a friendly and pleasant manner, continue to win the hearts of newcomers to the region.

This is Holderness, a very special place, populated with a very special people.

HOLDERNESS

Holderness is a thin strip
of land flanked by the River
Humber and the North Sea.
The numbers on this map refer
to the illustrations of each
village and town in the book.

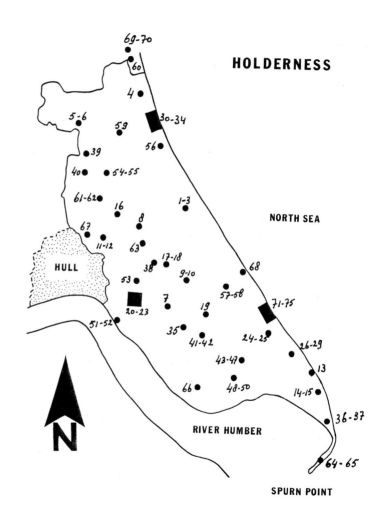

HOLDERNESS

Aldbrough

1   This is one of the villages under constant threat from the sea. It has been home to the Normans and Saxons, and is thought earlier to the Romans. The shrinking coastline has taken its toll, and it is thought that much of Aldbrough's history, including the first church, lies under the sea. This was built by a Saxon nobleman called Ulf. The picture shows Black House and its outbuildings. This postcard was sent in early 1918 by a soldier to his sweetheart, and tells how the soldiers were billeted there during the Great War.

BLACK HOUSE, ALDBORO'.

Aldbrough

2   This was the approach to the village in 1901. The distance between this road and the sea has been considerably diminished over the years.

Aldbrough

3   Like many Holderness villages the inhabitants were mainly farmworkers and their families, but there was also a brewery and brick and tile works which offered employment. The village had a good proportion of elegant and well-built houses. The picture is of Roseville, with a well-stocked rose garden and arches, setting a tradition which continues in the village to this day.

Atwick

4   This picturesque small village is situated just north of Hornsea. This view of Cliff Road earlier this century shows the village green with the remains of the old market cross just visible in the distance.

CLIFF ROAD, ATWICK.

Brandesburton

5   This group of pygmies was once a familiar sight around the village of Brandesburton. The celebrated Holderness explorer, Colonel J.J. Harrison of Brandesburton Hall, was responsible for bringing these diminutive negrilloes to England. In 1905 whilst in the Belgian Congo (now Zaire) Colonel Harrison obtained permission to bring back to England a small party of pygmies, whose names were Bokane (chief), Kuarke, Mongonga, Mafutiminga, Matuka and Amuriape. So much interest was shown in these exotic visitors that a tour of Music Halls around Britain was organised. After a two-year sojourn in England, with much time happily spent at Brandesburton where they had the complete run of the extensive woodland, the seven visitors were returned to their homes in the Congo. They sailed from Hull on 17 November 1907.

Brandesburton

6   This rare photograph, sadly damaged, shows one of Brandesburton's enduring celebrities. Little David, as the name implies, was a diminutive character who made his living as a coalman. He must have been quite a strong little man constantly heaving hundredweight sacks of coal from his makeshift cart, which was drawn by his faithful old horse.

Burstwick

7   In the nineteenth century, Methodism was dominant in Holderness. Many chapels were built in the area, surprisingly some funds were raised but loans were not unusual. There were two forms of Methodism favoured, the Wesleyan faith which had many supporters in trade, such as the shopkeeper and blacksmith. The Primitive Methodists, however, were mainly from the working classes. Burstwick Primitive Methodist Chapel was designed by the architect T.B. Thompson and opened in 1898.

Burton Constable

8   Burton Constable House has grown over the centuries from a tower of brick and stone, intended as a defence against the coastal raiders, to its present impressive dimensions. In 1570 it was decided to develop the building by adding rooms and another tower. At that time the Constable's principle seat was at Halsham.

The present building owes much of its charm to Timothy Lightowler, many of whose architectural drawings are still in the family collection. The landscaping of the gardens is primarily the work of Capability Brown, dating from the eighteenth century. Burton Constable was mentioned in the Domesday Book as Santriburtone, the present name having derived from the union of Erneburg de Burton and Ulbert le Constable.

Here the imposing front elevation with huntsmen and hounds gathered on the magnificent lawn.

The house is still the home of the Lord Paramount of the Seigniory of Holderness.

Burton Constable Hall.

Burton Pidsea

9   This view was taken about 1926 and shows a rather desolate wintry view of the village, which in the summer months is quite a pleasant place.

The celebrated antiquarian Robert Raines, who was born at Whitby, spent thirteen years of his life in Burton Pidsea, and learned to read and write at the village school. He later became a vicar and wrote several books. The family is commemorated in the fourteenth century church.

Burton Pidsea

10   In rural areas where villages were poor, a man often worked incredibly long hours to enable him to bring up his family. Sons traditionally joined their fathers working on the land, but it was considered very fortunate if a girl could secure a position in service 'at the big house'. These two young ladies, Miss Minnie Sizer and Miss Arksey, were in service at The Chestnuts, Burton Pidsea, in 1907.

Coniston

11   This has always been a small village. In the Domesday Book it is recorded as Coiningesbie. Basically in its early days it consisted of just one street and a few farms. This is a typical Holderness farm building. It is interesting to note the bicycle as the village has been described as almost a suburb of Hull, and was within easy cycling distance of Holderness Road.

Coniston

12   Almost anywhere in Holderness, and at any season of the year, scenes like this were a familiar sight. The patient horses were drawing either ploughs, harrows or carts of various types according to the task. These ladies at the Vinyard, Coniston, have obviously come along for the photograph, as unlike the men, they are not suitably dressed for work in the fields.

Dimlington

13   The 132 feet long *S.S. Dynamo* ran ashore at Dimlington near Easington on 19th January 1912. The trawler which was built by Cook, Welton & Gemmell at Beverley in 1905 for F. & T. Ross of Hull, was homeward-bound from the White Sea laden with some eight hundred kits of fish, valued at around £1,000. Fortunately there were no fatalaties, but contemporary reports in the local press expressed doubts about the possibility of refloating the vessel, declaring her to be in a curious position.

Easington

14   This village lies on the tapering strip of land leading to Kilnsea and Spurn. Like all the villages in this part of Holderness it has ancient traditions, the present church having celebrated the 800th anniversary of its foundation in 1990.

There has been an excellent school at Easington since the nineteenth century along with others in the surrounding villages some of which, such as Holmpton and Welwick, have now closed, leaving Easington to carry on the tradition of high-quality local education.

This little group of children from around the turn of the century, along with their teachers, appear to be from a cross section of family backgrounds.

Easington

15   One of the popular features of the village was Loten's Museum, a place filled with natural history specimens and many bizarre objects. Philip Loten, collector and curator of the museum, was an accomplished taxidermist, who mounted with much enthusiasm any dead creature he found in the area, including many unfortunates washed up on the nearby beaches. When his own dog Fido died, he was duly stuffed and mounted and given the place of honour amongst the exhibits. The more unusual, even maccabre, included the posies of flowers made from dead mens toenails, a bonnet made from used postage stamps, and bridal flower sprays made from fish scales. The Bombardment of Alexandria could be seen framed behind glass, the picture being made entirely of used beer bottle corks. Perhaps the most popular exhibit was his masterpiece, a representation in stuffed animals and birds of the old children's story 'Who Killed Cock Robin?' The whole story is reproduced in a series of tableaus, from the wedding and killing of Robin, the burial and final trial and execution of the sparrow. When Loten died in 1908, the museum passed into the hands of the Speight family, remaining open until around 1957. The entire contents of the place of curiosities were subsequently auctioned off in 1964 with just a few of pieces remaining in the area.

Ellerby

16   This village was mentioned in the Domesday Book as Alverdebi. Old Ellerby, like most of Holderness, was mainly agricultural and largely belonged to the Burton Constable Estate. Its inhabitants included the usual tradesmen such as the blacksmith, carpenter and wheelwright.

This was the original settlement, but with the coming of the railway to Hornsea, a few cottages and farms grew around New Ellerby.

Elstronwick

17   This is referred to as one of the smallest villages on the Plain of Holderness, and is known to locals as Elsternwick. It is a charming village with tiny cottages and farms, and a church near Humbleton Beck. This rather fragile looking wooden bridge joined it to neighbouring Danthorpe, before a more substantial structure was built in 1928.

Elstronwick

18   This heavily-laden waggon is about to set out from Elstronwick for the Primitive Methodist Sunday School outing in 1913. To many, both children and adults, this was one of the high spots of the year, with the destination being either Hornsea or Withernsea. There were boxes and hampers of food and other refreshments suitable for a picnic, and even the festively-trimmed horses enjoyed a rest and grazing in pastures new.

Halsham

19 The harvest is the climax of the year for the farmer. Methods of harvesting remained almost unchanged for centuries, the crops being cut with scythes and sickles. The scytheman worked to a steady rhythm, and it was not unusual to see as many as twenty men on the larger farms in a staggered row across a field sweeping together. Although the horse-drawn reaper was introduced in the late nineteenth century, there were still many farms, particularly the small tenant farms, where the scytheman still cut the harvest well into the twentieth century.

This man weilding a scythe in a field at Halsham is Mr. Leonard Sharp, one year after the finish of the Great War in 1919.

Hedon

20   St. Augustine's Church is
the focal point of this small
medieval market town, and is
rightly designated The King of
Holderness. This cruciform
church, which is chiefly thirteenth century, has a perpen-
dicular east window. The impressive central tower is
fifteenth century. St.
Augustine's Church has always played a large part in the
spiritual affairs of the town-
folk.

St. Augustine's Church, Hedon

Hedon

21 An interesting view of Market Place taken around the turn of the century. The old cobbled road is clearly defined. This was characteristic of the old town of Hedon, and whilst there are some examples still to be seen in the town, sadly they are slowly being covered over the years. The public house on the left is the Dog and Duck, which was closed in 1916.

Hedon

22   The Horse Well at Hedon traces its origins back to the middle ages. It is thought to have had a ducking stool to deal with scolds and shrewish women in the manner of the times. Local opinion, however, supports the theory that its main use was for watering horses and cattle.

Hedon

23   Although it was not within the town boundary, the racecourse, which was only a few minutes walk from the town centre, was known to the racing fraternity as Hedon Park, being on the north side of Hedon Road from Hull.

In the early 1880's the East Riding Race Course Ltd Company was formed. The course was officially opened in 1888 having cost in the region of £75,000. On the following day a crowd of 20,000 attended the first meeting. Its fortunes varied, and in 1909 it was declared bankrupt, its assets being used to pay debts. It was used by the army in the Great War, but in the 1920's the stands were demolished and the land was sold to Hull City Council who still own it.

Hollym

24   Hollym House was built in 1774 and in 1787 it was bought by the Reverend Robert Barker, and in 1816 was passed to his sons Edmund and Charles. Charles, like his father, was a clergyman and stayed as Vicar of Hollym for forty years.

It was a very grand house in a beautiful setting with a coach house, stables and a conservatory. Unfortunately in later years the house fell into disrepair and was demolished in 1988.

Hollym

25   In 1754 there were two
public houses in Hollym, but
now only the Plough Inn remains. The oldest part of the
building is thought to have
been built almost four hundred years ago. One of the
walls which can still be seen
was built of cow dung and
straw, many of the later bricks
were made at the Hollym
Brickworks, which closed
many years ago.

Holmpton

26   The name derives from the earlier Holmtune of Norman times. Its meaning is 'Town of the Holm' a holm being an area of low flat-land, often a river meadow. One of the features of Holmpton is the abundance of trees in comparison to other areas of Holderness, due, no doubt, to the foresight of the Lords of the manor, Holmpton Hall, during the eighteenth and nineteenth centuries. The village is founded on a ridge of boulder clay perilously near to the sea. It is largely eighteenth century and tales are told of tunnels from some houses to the church. Theories about these vary from fanciful smugglers tales, to suggestions of secret worship during the days of religious persecution. Holmpton has always been an agricultural village, Bumble Bee Farm later became West Farm and in 1936 was bought by a Mr. Herd, along with Manor Farm and North Farm. These he gave to his three sons making them one of the largest farming families in the area.

Holmpton

27   The Holmpton Rocket Life Saver Crew and equipment returning to base after rescuing sailors from a vessel which had run aground north of the Old Hive in 1935. The lifesaver crew were issued with a rocket firing device which could project a lifeline out to a ship in trouble at sea. Attached to this line were stronger lines equipped with a Breeches Buoy for use by the seamen to be hauled ashore. The members of the rocket crew were, from left to right: leader Bob Branton, George Langthorp, coastguard Ling, Johnny Gell, Theodore Clubley and George Billaney.

Holmpton

28   The camp by the road between Holmpton and Withernsea provided very reasonably-priced holiday accommodation for families earlier this century. The group of people above are obviously enjoying the amenity, which was also used by larger bodies of people such as youth organisations and the like.

Holmpton

29   The road leading out of Holmpton runs to Out Newton. This tiny hamlet has to some extent disappeared into the sea. One landmark which for many years stood on the very edge of the cliffs was finally claimed by the sea over fifty years ago.

Outnewton Road, Holmpton, E. Yorks.
Lister's Series 1852.

Hornsea

30   The Granville Court Hotel was built in 1912. There is evidence which indicates that it stood on land which had formerly been an Anglo Saxon burial ground.

In the early part of this century there was a great interest in the use of water as a health cure, the Granville had all facilities for this and was known in some circles as the Hornsea Hydro. It had large ballrooms and luxurious accommodation which attracted many visitors. Soldiers were billeted there during both world wars.

Sadly over the years its popularity waned and it was converted into flats. It was later severely damaged by fire, and the now derelict building was demolished in 1990.

Hornsea

31   Sherwood's Gardens were situated on Newbegin. There were amazing formal flower beds like the above illustration, which along with plants which provided a kaleidoscope of colour, were edged and decorated with a multitude of small colourful stones and sea shells. At the southern end of the garden there was a very ornate arch, beneath which stood the statue of a man clad in full highland dress. Later it became known as Tansley Gardens. Mr. Tansley, who was a greengrocer, also grew vegetables, which he regularly picked for the customers to his shop.

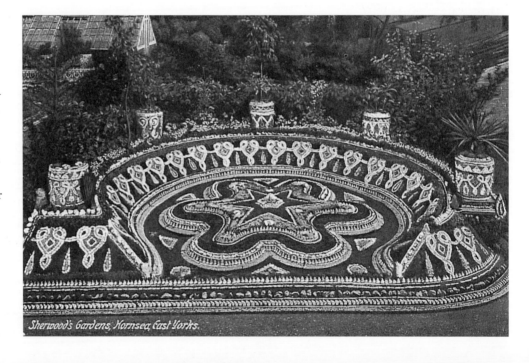

Sherwood's Gardens, Hornsea, East Yorks.

Hornsea

32 Harry Russell was born in 1877. During his teenage years he gained much useful theatrical experience and played the Music Halls with such top artistes as Dan Leno, George Robey and Kate Collins. He first produced a pierrot show in Plymouth, but came back to his beloved north country where Harry Russells Cadets and Concert Party proved a great success in Hornsea in 1907. His troupe appeared for several seaons in the town, where they were very popular with tourist and townsfolk alike. Harry, the gentleman seated far right, often referred in later years to this period in Hornsea as being the happiest time of his life.

HARRY RUSSELLS CADETS AND CONCERT PARTY

Hornsea

33   This poignant picture was taken in 1929, it shows the devastating effect of the waves upon the groynes and sea defences at Hornsea.

The Sentinels, Hornsea

Hornsea

34   One of the town's most endearing characters was Rose Carr (1843-1913). A great lover of horses, Rose followed the occupation of a carrier and was a familiar figure at the Hornsea railway station as she waited for the trains from Hull. Rose was a heavily-built woman of immense strength, with abundant anecdotes relating to this fact. It was said she could carry a sixteen stone sack of corn under each arm at the same time. Her immense feats of strength led many people to question her gender, a fact which was still not made clear at her death. In her youth she was kicked in the face by an animal, probably a horse, which left her badly disfigured. Despite her rough manners and formidable appearance Rose was highly respected in the area, and was responsible for many acts of kindness.

Keyingham

35   In the Domesday Book the village is recorded as Caingeham, thought to have derived from Caega, who established an early settlement there. Like most of Holderness, agriculture has always been the main occupation. The main street seen here is now a very busy road linking Hull with Easington, Spurn and Withernsea. It would appear that everyone has paused in his or her pursuits for the benefit of the photographer.

KEYINGHAM E YORKS W&S HULL

Kilnsea

36   Kilnsea, being low lying, was particularly vulnerable to flooding. Some of the worst floods recorded in the area appear to have been around the month of March, which meant that crops which were just beginning to sprout were destroyed, sometimes bringing ruin to the helpless farmers.

This is the flood of 12th March 1900, being viewed no doubt with despair by men on the Easington Road. In 1906, Mr. Stanley Wilson MP, was expressing to the Board of Trade the urgent need for adequate sea defences.

Kilnsea

37 Dr. William Henry Coates was what can only be described as a 'character'. He lived at Bleak House in High Street, Patrington, and was a doctor, surgeon, barrister, county councillor and clerk to the Parish Council. He was a great supporter of the Liberal Party, and being a philanthropist was highly regarded for his charitable acts, which included organising garden parties for disabled and deprived children.

For recreation the doctor had a beach chalet at Kilnsea, where as here in 1906 he entertained his friends. Dr. Coates is the gentleman in the white cap in the front row. Apparently he was a great organiser and involved all present in the preparation of meals and general running of the chalet.

He died in 1924 at the early age of 55, a tragic loss to the area, and sadly mourned by all who knew him.

Lelley

38   Lelley Mill was renowned for the fact that if there was very little wind the sails would turn whilst those of its neighbours in the surrounding area would remain motionless.

There was a small post mill on the site as early as 1712, but in succeeding years with various tenants it was developed until the early part of this century when this magnificent structure dominated the flat surrounding area. The mill is now a derelict tower without sails.

Leven

39   The agricultural shows
which took place between the
end of harvesting and the
Martinmas hirings were ea-
gerly anticipated by man,
woman and child. There were
entertainments of every type,
but one of the most popular
events was the judging of the
horses and carts. Here we see
the proud waggoner with his
highly-groomed and be-
decked charge.

Long Riston

40   A wedding was always a time for rejoicing in a village. If the happy couple were gentry, a half day holiday was sometimes granted and perhaps a free tea would be provided in the village hall. This picture of the newly-weds leaving the church in 1908 shows the ladies of the village each wearing their finery for the occasion. The men are noticable by their absence, if not working the half day holiday, it would prove a grand excuse to celebrate in the local pub.

LEAVING CHURCH.   NO3
JACKSON-JACKSON WEDDING. LONG RISTON AUG 11th 1908.

Ottringham

41   This Holderness village on the main road from Hull to the coast is approximately fourteen miles east of Hull and eight miles west of Withernsea. The church of St. Wilfrid, around which the village clusters, is mainly fourteenth century, and is visible over much of the Holderness Plain, having an impressive spire in excess of a hundred feet.

This peaceful scene around 1920, is much changed today, with a constant stream of vehicular traffic both to and from the coast. It is in the heart of a farming community and is one of the few villages which has largly escaped the attention of the developers.

Ottringham near Hull.   "Scott" Series No. 498

Ottringham

42　A peaceful rural scene with beasts grazing away from the busy village. St. Wilfrid's Church dominates the skyline, as indeed it does in other views of the immediate area. There is an air of timelessness and serenity about the picture, which is typical of much of Holderness even today. The photograph dates from the early 1920's.

ST. WILFRIDS CH, OTTRINGHAM. E. YORKS. W&S

Patrington

43   The village is graced by arguably one of the finest parish churches in Britain. Deservedly named 'The Queen of Holderness' St. Patrick's is a cathedral in miniature. This cruciform church of great beauty has a magnificent central tower on which a tall spire emerges from an open corona. This lofty landmark dominates the south Holderness area, and on a clear day can be seen in south Lincolnshire. Almost entirely in the Decorated Style, the church owes a great deal to the skills of Robert Paryk, a master mason of York Minster, who helped with the design. It is mostly fourteenth century, being built before the Black Death.

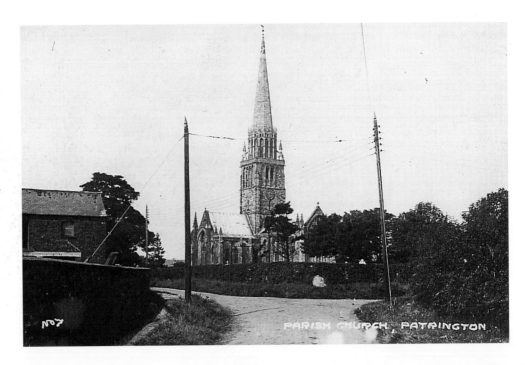

PARISH CHURCH, PATRINGTON

Patrington

44 Patrington Market Place was the scene of an annual custom which has long been abandoned in the Holderness area. On Martinmas Day (23rd November) each year, Holderness farm lads congregated to offer themselves for hire to the farmers for the next years work. When a bargain was struck the farmer gave the new lad a 'fest', a small sum of money, once the farmhand accepted this he had bonded himself for a year's labour for a fixed wage.

Patrington

45   The Union Workhouse, a very small portion of which can be seen to the left of the picture, was built in 1838 to accommodate people from Paull to Spurn and inland as far as Burstwick. In 1904 the infirmary, which was a hospital wing, was built at right angles to the main building, its curved bay window at the far right surveyed the Patrington, Winestead road. It was known locally as 'The Workhouse' up to its closure in 1948. Subsequently the building became a factory, but was finally demolished in 1981.

Patrington

46 In 1854 the Hull and Holderness Railway was opened, linking Patrington to Hull and Withernsea. Not only did this provide extra employment in the village, but also made ammenities like the conveyance of milk to Hull, and delivery of goods to the villages much easier. The Railway Station, along with ticket office, proudly boasted a ladies' waiting room. There was living accommodation for the station master and his family. The staff can be distinguished from the people waiting for the train by their watch chains.

Patrington

47 Many of the men of Patrington lost their lives in the Great War. These worthy sons of the village are remembered on a memorial tablet in St. Patrick's Church. It was also decided that a fitting tribute would be a Roll of Honour to be erected on the village green. This was unveiled at a military ceremony on 10th November 1917, one year almost to the day before the Armistice was signed on 11th November 1918. Because of the timing, some men who served and some men who were taken prisoner are not named on the memorial.

PATRINGTON ROLL OF HONOUR.

Patrington Haven

48   Agriculture and fishing were the main occupations of the Haven, nearby Sunk Island, providing work for some, the chief fishing family being the Parrotts, who originally worked from a small harbour, but in 1888 they moved to Stone Creek. Taken around the turn of the century, this group of children standing across the main street appear to be almost bemused by the photographer.

Patrington Haven

49   Haven Mill was built in 1810 and at the turn of this century was occupied by Ronald Cuthbert, whose family were millers at Easington. The mill boasted a steam engine for when their was not enough wind to provide power to drive the massive sails.

The mill was working and producing animal feed until 1937.

Patrington Haven

50 The people in the photograph are gathered outside the Patrington Haven Primitive Methodist Chapel which was built in 1905.

The occasion was the unveiling of the War Memorial to those from the village who gave their lives in the Great War.

Paull

51   The village of Paull is situated on the banks of the River Humber about seven miles east of Kingston Upon Hull. It was once important for its shipbuilding, including impressive gunboats, perhaps the best known being the Anson, which was launched in 1812.

Paull also boasts coastguard cottages and a small lighthouse, now a private residence. The main street (this picture) was built mainly in the nineteenth century. The Humber Tavern on the left was built in 1808 and The Crown, right, in 1865. Note the brewery delivery lorry outside the premises.

Paull

52   This dignified house is typical of the type of property offered by the church to its country vicars. It may appear to be a large establishment for one man and his family but it was expected that the vicar would have a wife and a variable number of children and, as was the practice in Victorian days, he would have come from a good family and be accustomed to a decent standard of living, which meant accommodating servants. It was also customary for an unmarried curate to be part of the vicarage household.

Paull. The Vicarage. No.11.

Preston

53 Founded during the Anglo Saxon invasions, the village is mentioned in the Domesday Book. The name means 'Priest Town'. Stage coaches passed through the village on the Hull-Patrington journey in later centuries. During the nineteenth century it was one of the principle pig producing areas in East Yorkshire.

Preston also had two corn mills of great significance to the area, but nothing remains of them today.

The church seen in the distance is All Saints' which is mainly Early English in style. This peaceful scene is a far cry from today's constant stream of traffic through this busy village.

PRESTON, NEAR HULL.

Rise

54   The village of Rise, as the name implies, was built on high or rising ground. The church, All Saints', is in the fourteenth century style and is built on the edge of the park of Rise Hall, the home of the Bethell family. In 1845 Richard Bethell restored the church, which contains numerous monuments to the Bethell family, including Christopher Bethell, who was killed at Mafeking, and five members of the family who were killed in the Great War.

RISE CHURCH,
Nr. Hull.

"SCOTT" SERIES. No. 733.

Rise

55 In 1910 Captain G.R. Bethell of Rise Hall contested the Parliamentary Seat for Holderness against Mr. Stanley Wilson. Captain Bethell came from a family which had a long record of representing Yorkshire in Parliament. As the vignettes on his campaign voting card show, the cause of the agricultural workers was his manifesto.

GENERAL ELECTION, 1910.

VOTE FOR

BETHELL

THE

LABOURER'S FRIEND,

AND

PEACE

AND

PLENTY.

inted and Published by Hudson & Son, Edmund St. & Livery St., Birmingham.

Rolston

56   One of the high spots of the year for the Orderly Boys was their annual summer camp. The contingent on this picture being conveyed by Hull Corporation Road Works lorries are approaching Rolston in 1920.

The Orderly Boys were formed in 1919 by Harry Baxter, an ex Staff Sergeant in the Yorks & Lancs Regiment. His idea was to give poor boys something to do. They helped to clean the streets of Hull for a token payment, and held parades wearing smart uniforms. During the camp visits they were treated like territorials and were finally disbanded in 1939.

Roos

57 All Saints' Church at Roos has a most striking approach. The path, flanked by yew trees, leads to an impressive stone staircase. Behind the porch at the end of the walk rises the fifteenth century tower. The porch has three arches, and the nave has impressive thirteenth century arcades. The chantry was built in the fourteenth and fifteenth centuries.

Roos Church, Withernsea.

Roos

58   Roos is a very old village, there were settlements in the area long before the Romans. The name is thought to be Friesian in origin from a word meaning 'wet lands'. Like its neighbours, Roos has always been a farming community surrounded by fields. These charming little Merry Milkmaids echo the agricultural theme with their pails and milking stools. They appear to have been popular entertainers, as they are known to have appeared at various social functions.

MERRY MILKMAIDS
ROOS, AUGUST 1904.

Seaton

59   Seaton is a small village about three miles from the coast near Hornsea. It has changed little over the years. Much of the farming in the Holderness area relied heavily on horses such as this magnificent specimen pictured with Andrew at Seaton in 1893.

Skipsea

60   This village lies perilously near to the North Sea, which is a continuous threat. William the Conqueror gave the Isle of Holderness to a knight called Drogo de Bevere, who built his castle on Skipsea Brough. Many of the older houses are built of cobbles from the beach. Like the rest of the area it is, and has long been, a farming community.

The War Memorial was built to honour the men of the village who gave their lives in the Great War of 1914-1918.

War Memorial, Skipsea.

Skirlaugh

61   The village was mentioned in the Domesday Book as Skirelai. The Old English 'scir' means a cut or divide, and 'lai' was a lake or beck. The village is aptly named as it is split into north and south Skirlaugh by the Lambwath Stream.

The magnificent noble towered church of St. Augustine was built between 1401 and 1405 by Walter Skirlaw, the then Bishop of Durham, who, it has been suggested, took his name from the village. There were two Lords of the Manor, for the north it was William Bethell, and for the south Sir F.A. Clifford Constable.

In the late nineteenth century Skirlaugh was a thriving community with various trades and occupations represented as well as farmers. Perhaps the most interesting was a taxidermist. The Workhouse was eventually taken over by Holderness Rural District Council, and is still used as the offices of Holderness Borough Council.

Skirlaugh

62   Annie Croft was born at Skirlaugh on 7th August 1896. She 'began' her stage career when she won the third prize in a singing contest at the age of six. Annie studied with Madame Sharrah at Hull School of Music, and at the age of ten years organised her first concert and began teaching dancing. She made her London debut at the Shaftsbury Theatre in August 1914, succeeding Cicely Courtnage as Phylis in 'The Cinema Star'. Annie Croft reached the top of her profession in the 1930's playing in the West End of London in several productions.

Sproatley

63   In 1733 Mrs. Bridget Briggs left properties in her will, the rents from which were to build a schoolhouse for ten poor boys and ten poor girls of Sproatley. Other children could attend, but were obliged to pay for their education at the establishment. Sometimes money was provided to find boys an apprenticeship and girls jobs in service, and also to clothe them suitably for their employment.

A new school was built around 1870. Although there is now a modern school for five to eleven years olds, the charity continues to provide extras, and in some cases grants.

The photograph of the girls engaged in scarfe drill was taken in 1907.

Scarf Drill.
Sproatley Endowed school, 1907.
Lister's Series

Spurn Head

64   One theory is that this natural land formation is composed of sand and shingle washed down the east coast by the sea to form a peninsula which is partially sheltered by the Humber estuary. It is constantly threatened by the North Sea and has been breached on more than one occasion, a really serious breach occurring as a result of the great gales of 1849. It has always presented a threat to mariners, and several lighthouses have been built with varying success. The one shown above was built from 1893 to 1895. The flash of the light came at fifteen second intervals and is said to have been visible in excess of fifteen miles in clear weather. The peninsula has for many years had a lifeboat station which has a long and distinguished history, with brave crews and amazing rescues, the men and their families living, as they still do, on this thin spit of land.

Spurn Head.

Spurn

65   Fred Stephenson was the
Spurn postman in the 1920's.
He is seen here riding his bicycle on the flooded road
between Spurn and Kilnsea.
He later rode a motorbike and
sidecar on his rounds and
eventually graduated to a van,
which, considering the type
of weather he encountered in
winter, must have proved a
blessing.

Sunk Island

66   No other place in Yorkshire can compare with Sunk Island. It is reminiscent of Holland where the polders, like Sunk Island, were reclaimed from the sea. On the edge of Holderness it is flanked by the River Humber on one side and by the villages of Keyingham, Ottringham and Patrington. 'Sunk' has always been a farming community whose air of peace and tranquility and timelessness captured the imagination of the novelist Winifred Holtby, who took her inspiration for 'Cold Harbour Colony' in her novel 'South Riding' from this area. In the second half of the seventeenth century, silt deposits from the Humber were reclaimed at the instigation of one Anthony Gilby. After the Great War, the Ministry of Agriculture instituted a resettlement scheme for 'discharged soldiers and others' which became Sunk Island Crown Colony. Sadly the scheme did not come up to expectations. The new tenants of the cottages were mostly men from urban backgrounds, with no experience of farming, and many were frankly unsuited to the bucolic lifestyle. The photograph shows the back view of one of the cottages with pigsty. The family were some of the earliest settlers in 1918. There were some, however, who proved successful and stayed with the project, but they had a very hard time in the early years, and many eventually abandoned the colony after a short trial.

Swine

67   The village of Swine is dominated by the imposing church of St. Mary. Built during the twelfth century, it was from 1154 a Cistercian Nunnery until the Dissolution of the Monasteries in 1539 by Henry VIII. The name of the village is thought to derive from a Saxon King Swaine, who was buried there. But in all probability the name refers to its importance as a pig market from the Old English 'swin' meaning swine. Holderness is still renowned for its large-scale pig production.

Inside the church are many interesting features including medieval woodcarvings. This carving is known locally as 'The Winking nun'. Dating from the mid-fourteenth century, it depicts the head of a woman partially concealed by a cowl, who appears to be winking. The creatures at either side are hares, symbolic of fertility and lasciviousness.

Tunstall

68   Tunstall is said to have the highest percentage of cobbled buildings in the area. Throughout England cobbled buildings are very rare. Many of those in the hamlet were constructed during the eighteenth and nineteenth centuries, when other building material was not easy to procure. Cobbles were brought up from the beach and cliffs as erosion took place. Obviously this practice has long been carried out in the Holderness area. All Saints' Church as can be seen clearly shows the cobbles. There was a church on the site in 1115, but much of the present church dates from the fifteenth century. Tunstall is another village which is under constant threat from the hungry sea.

ALL SAINTS CHURCH, TUNSTALL

Ulrome

69   Like other places with coastal access, Ulrome, near Skipsea, had a Coastguard Station with men always on the alert to help distressed vessels at sea.

The Holderness coast, due to its exposure to the rugged elements, appears to have had a high percentage of marine disasters.

COASTGUARD STATION, ULROME.

Ulrome

70   A scene which is very typical of Holderness, with a village pond and tree-lined roads. Perhaps this charming little girl is waiting for the gentleman cycling along the road.

ULROME.

Withernsea

71   The east coast town of
Withernsea was affectionately
referred to as Hull's Holiday
Town. Renowned for its sandy
beaches and bracing air, local
businessman Anthony Bannis-
ter realised the potential of a
rail service from Hull, linking
the villages en route to Withernsea. His railway was finally
opened on 26th June 1854.
This picture, taken in the
1920's, shows part of Queen
Street in an unfamiliar view to
the summer visitors. In winter conditions Withernsea in
the past has been completely
isolated by heavy falls of snow
which form huge drifts, ren-
dering the approach roads
impassable.

Withernsea

72   Since the first Methodist meeting was held in a cottage, and the first Methodist Chapel built on Hull Road in 1875, the chapel has always had a strong support in Withernsea. The church on the right is the Wesleyan Church, which was built on the corner of Queen Street and Young Street in 1900. It was demolished in the 1960's to make way for a block of flats which were named Wesley Court. Young Street was also built around the turn of the century, a quiet cul-de-sac of typical Victorian terraced houses, as seen in 1910. The Band Stand which faces the promenade was once a popular feature with visitors and residents alike, but it no longer exists.

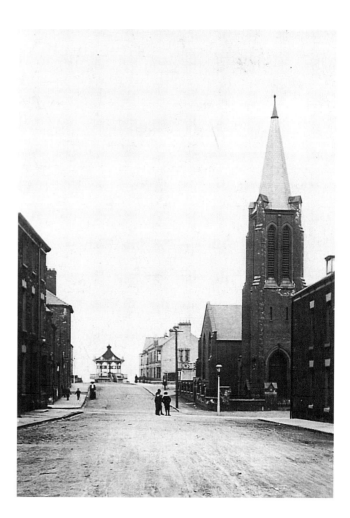

Withernsea

73   Naylor's popular gift shop at the corner of Queen Street and Hull Road where 'watch and clock and jewellery repairs were done by experienced workmen'. On the right is Kirk's, slater and glazier, and further down is the high roof of the Hull Road Methodist Church which was built in 1879. The lighthouse dominates the scene. It was built in 1892-1893 taking some eighteen months to build. The tall octagonal tower which has always been painted white, is built of brick and concrete. The lighthouse is now the town museum.

Withernsea

74   In the 1920's Withernsea Carnival became a holiday attraction. It is usually held at the beginning of August. This is part of the parade moving along Queen Street in 1927. Fancy dress was the order of the day, both for residents and visitors. The Carnival King and Queen crowning ceremony usually taking place in front of the castellated pier towers.

Withernsea

75   The relentless sea pounding the Promenade at Withernsea. Scenes of this nature have been photographed since late Victorian times, including the demolition of the Pier.

The situation today is that the force of the waves has inflicted severe damage to the wall and measures are in hand to halt the erosion.

ROUGH SEA WITHERNSEA   4